GALAXY OF SUPERSTARS

Ben Affleck

Backstreet Boys

Garth Brooks

Mariah Carey

Cameron Diaz

Leonardo DiCaprio

Tom Hanks

Hanson

Jennifer Love Hewitt

Lauryn Hill

Ewan McGregor

Mike Myers

'N Sync

LeAnn Rimes

Britney Spears

Spice Girls

Jonathan Taylor Thomas

Venus Williams

CHELSEA HOUSE PUBLISHERS

CONTENTS

1

ROCKING AT
VENICE HIGH

Venice High School in Los Angeles, California, is situated on Venice Boulevard, less than two miles from Santa Monica Bay. The old school building, built in 1914, provided the perfect location for a Britney Spears video shoot.

The beachfront community of Venice was founded in 1900 by an entrepreneurial man named Abbot Kinney. Kinney had the idea to make a city similar to Venice, Italy, complete with 16 miles of canals, gondolas, and singing gondoliers. After a great deal of hard work, and not without a host of problems, he realized his vision. Later Venice became a part of Los Angeles and developed into more of a resort and residential community.

Mr. Kinney would have been quite surprised to hear the singing that sounded forth in the hallways of Venice High School one hot summer day in 1998. It was certainly nothing like what he would have heard from his ballad-crooning gondoliers. The up-and-coming bright new star, 16-year-old Britney Spears, was happy with the selection of the old school building.

Britney wasn't the first star to be rocking in the halls

Britney and her dancers give an enthusiastic performance. A seasoned entertainer, she has been in front of audiences since she was two years old.

of old Venice High. The school was made famous in 1973 when it was chosen as the location for the smash musical hit *Grease.* As Rydell High, the building was seen by millions of viewers all over the world in one of the most popular movies ever made.

Britney felt that a school would be the ideal setting for her new song, "Baby One More Time." Back in New York, when she first saw what the video director had developed on the story board, she didn't like his idea at all.

"They had this really bizarre video idea, this animated Power Ranger-y thing," she said. Knowing kids as only a teenager can, she stated her protest. "This isn't right," she told the executives. "If you want me to reach four-year-olds, then OK. But if you want me to reach my age group . . ."

Britney's idea was to feature a classroom setting where kids dressed in Catholic school uniforms were "bored out of our minds." It was also her suggestion to tie up their blouses and wear short skirts and knee-highs. "I want something all the kids my age can relate to. They're bored. They want to get out of school and dance." Her idea was accepted and the location was chosen.

Britney, who hails from the tiny town of Kentwood, Louisiana, has never had a problem meeting people. In fact, she makes new friends wherever she goes. But it was still comforting to have her traveling companion, Felicia Culotta, and her cousin, Chad Spears, involved in the video shoot. Felicia, a family friend, was given the role of the teacher in the classroom. Cousin Chad, who also modeled for Abercrombie & Fitch, was cast as her love

interest and was seen sitting on the bleachers in the gymnasium scene.

Excitement filled the air as the troupe arrived in front of Venice High School and began to unload all the equipment. Since it was June, only a handful of summer school students were in the building. The makeup

A scene from the movie Grease. *Venice High School in California, which was used as the movie's fictional Rydell High School, was also the setting of Britney's video,* Baby One More Time.

artists began working their magic before the filming could begin. Following the makeup session, Britney's light brown hair was plaited in two simple braids.

As with a movie, the scenes for the music video were not filmed in sequence. The random-order shooting made it easier, but the video still required three days of hard work. To Britney it didn't seem like work. It was the best experience of her young life. "It was like everyone was there working for me and it was so cool. Everyone was so nice."

When the music kicked in and the girls broke loose from their classroom boredom, lively dancing erupted in the halls, the gym, and even the parking lot of Venice High. Having been an award-winning gymnast, as well as a talented dancer, Britney performed with ease all the back flips and other tricks required for the scenes.

The lyrics, Britney explained, are about a girl who has broken up with her boyfriend and now is sorry. She wants him back again.

> Oh baby baby
> Oh baby baby
> Oh baby baby
> How was I suppose to know
> That something wasn't right here. . . .
> My loneliness is killing me (and I)
> I must confess I still believe (still believe)
> When I'm not with you I lose my mind
> Please give me a sign
> Hit me baby one more time. . . .

The song may appear light and sugary, but the lyrics do not truly reflect the amount of hard work the young singer has put in to reach her goals. Britney Spears is in no way an overnight sensation.

"I've been working toward this moment for a long time," she thoughtfully remarked in a recent interview. How long could a "long time" be to a 16-year-old? It could be 14 years, if you begin when you're only two!

2

BORN
TO SING

Kentwood, Louisiana, the birthplace of Britney Jean Spears, is situated near the Mississippi-Louisiana border, an hour north of New Orleans. Boasting a population of about 2,500, Kentwood is a sleepy little community that hasn't changed much in the last couple of decades. A little way from Kentwood, Tangipahoa Parish, are open pastures where dairy cattle graze. Neatly tended dairy farms dot the landscape.

Motorists who approach the small town of Kentwood today are greeted by a welcome sign that says "Spears County," in recognition of Britney's newfound fame. However, when Britney was born on December 2, 1981, her arrival caused a wave of excitement only among the Spears families—of which there are several in the area. Aunts and uncles, cousins and grandparents, all live in the surrounding neighborhoods and are intensely interested in family affairs and concerns.

Britney was born into an ordinary middle-class home in the heart of the deep South. Jamie Spears, Britney's father, owned a health club for a time, then worked as a building

---

Every time Britney sings, she fulfills her childhood dream of performing. When she was only two years old, Britney spent hours singing with a pretend microphone in front of the bathroom mirror.

contractor. Mother Lynne spent years as a school teacher. Britney's brother Bryan, five years her senior, was the typical protective, yet teasing, older brother while they were growing up. Younger sister Jamie Lynne didn't appear on the scene until Britney was eight.

Britney cannot remember a time when she didn't dream of singing. And in her case, she did much more than just dream. At the tender age of two, she would apply her mother's makeup, stand in front of the bathroom mirror, pretend the hairbrush was a microphone, and sing to her heart's content. While the noise irritated her older brother, Britney's mother sensed that her daughter displayed real talent at this young age.

Twenty miles south of Kentwood, in the town of Hammond, Louisiana, there was a dance school called Renee Rusciano Donewar's School of Dance. Lynne Spears knew that every week the dance teacher, Renee Donewar, drove up to Kentwood to conduct dance classes in the Kentwood Community Center. When Britney turned three, Lynne enrolled her in Donewar's dance school.

"Britney was a real leader," Renee related, recalling those early classes. "Young as she was, if another child could not get a certain step, Britney was quick to assist and show that student how it went."

Britney studied under Renee for about three years. Even though she was a quick study and always caught on to the steps more quickly than the others, this natural ability didn't give her an over-inflated ego.

"Britney was well-liked," Renee pointed out. "She got along well with all the other students."

Renee has a video of a three-year-old Britney performing a song and dance number to the

These little girls are already experienced dancers. Like them, Britney began studying dance at an early age— and her recent videos show off her natural ability.

tune of "Sophisticated Baby." "She had such cute facial expressions," Renee said with a chuckle. "It's priceless."

Being a teacher herself, Lynne Spears knew the importance of a quality education, and that's what she and her husband, Jamie, wanted for their children. They chose Parklane Academy, a private Christian school in McComb, Mississippi, dedicated to providing quality education with high standards of academic excellence. When her parents enrolled Britney in first grade at Parklane, Bryan was already a student there.

Parklane was 25 miles north of Kentwood. It drew students from four or five surrounding counties and enrollment fluctuated between 900 and 1,000 students in kindergarten through 12th grade. While the school was not affiliated with one certain church, the students were required to stand every morning for a devotional moment and a time of prayer. The school provided

Bible classes and boasted an active Bible club. This was the kind of firm foundation Jamie and Lynne wanted for their children.

In the spring of Britney's first-grade year, she won a competition at the Kentwood Dairy Festival with a song and dance number. This gave her the privilege of riding on the back of a convertible in the town parade, wearing her dance costume, and waving to the crowd. Other talent contests were to follow, which accustomed her to taking home the top prizes. Performing seemed to be second nature to her.

Close on the heels of dance class came gymnastics classes. Britney wasn't one to ask for something and then quit when the going got rough—she was willing to work hard and practice. She took to gymnastics as eagerly as she had to dance class, winning several competitions. In the car en route to gymnastics lessons, she listened to tapes of her favorite singing stars, Mariah Carey and Whitney Houston, and mimicked every note.

One summer Britney attended Bela Karolyi's gymnastics camp, which was situated on 500 acres in Huntsville, Texas. Karolyi, the world's most successful gymnastics coach, has coached such winners as Mary Lou Retton and Kerri Strug. Karolyi's summer camp was open to female gymnasts from seven years old and up. Campers received intensive training, with one coach for every five or six gymnasts. Each day there were six full hours of workouts—three in the morning and three in the afternoon.

The week-long camp included plenty of fun and games in addition to hard work. Like any good summer camp, fun times included swimming, canoeing, horseback riding, and campfire suppers, interspersed with funny skits and

World-renowned gymnastics coach Bela Karolyi gives encouragement to a young pupil. Britney attended gymnastics camp taught by Karolyi but later gave up the sport to concentrate on her dancing.

contests. Here Britney met many new friends while she perfected her routines.

The campers worked all week on one final routine, which was performed on the last day in front of visitors, parents, and coaches. Mr. Karolyi personally gave out special awards at the close of the camp.

In spite of all the perks from being a good gymnast, Britney would later leave the sport behind to concentrate more on dancing. She explained by saying, "In gymnastics, I could do a half, you know the twisty things, but I couldn't do a double. So that's when I quit."

Throughout the entire history of child stars— whether on stage, screen, or television—there have been many unhappy stories of "starstruck" mothers pushing their children to perform. The term "stage mother" is considered a very unflattering term. Lynne Spears was never this type of parent. On the contrary, it was Britney who was begging to enter pageants, talent contests, and gymnastic competitions. Fortunately, both of Britney's parents were willing to do whatever it took to allow their daughter every opportunity. Their sacrifices and support made it possible for Britney to follow her dreams.

"I was always the one telling my mom, 'I want to go to gymnastics. I want to go to vocal lessons,'" Britney told reporters later. "I'm just so thankful they were so supportive. . . . They knew this is what I wanted to do and they went that extra mile to support me."

Mary Ellen Chamberlin, the music teacher at Parklane, was known for presenting major musical productions each year. When Britney was in second grade, the production was entitled *Give Thanks America.* Britney played the part of the schoolmarm in the pioneer one-room schoolhouse. "The singing parts went to the older students," Mrs. Chamberlin said, "but I remember how cute Britney looked in her costume."

The next year, however, Britney sang the song "Lavender Blue" in the production *The Rainbow Connection.* It was during this third-grade year that family and friends were coming to realize that Britney truly had singing talent.

"Hers was a very commercial voice," Mrs. Chamberlin explained, "not the normal child voice. She was very much in control. Her range was limited, but she had a strong voice."

When Britney started third grade at Parklane, her teacher, Darlene Hughes, had already been teaching that class for 13 years. Mrs. Hughes's daughter, Robbey, was also in the same classroom that year. Britney and Robbey were the same age and remained friends all through their childhood years. And Mrs. Hughes also became a close family friend. "She's our baby," Mrs. Hughes said about Britney after her success had come full force. "I watched her grow up."

In the latter part of Britney's third-grade year, Jamie and Lynne had made contacts in New York City and learned that auditions were being held for the off-Broadway play *Ruthless*. They decided to take Britney to the Big Apple for an auditions. By this time a baby sister, Jamie Lynne, was born. But that didn't slow things down a bit. The baby was packed up and taken along to the city.

Mrs. Hughes remembers supplying Britney and her mother with a packet of lesson plans. That way there would be no lapse in her school work while Britney made treks back and forth to New York City.

"Britney did her homework, minded her own business, and made excellent grades—all As and Bs," Mrs. Hughes recalled, "and did a good job of keeping up with her lessons while away."

While the auditions went well, it would be a matter of months before the casting process for *Ruthless* was completed.

Back in Kentwood, during an event at Park-lane known as Grandparents' Day, Britney was called upon to perform the national anthem a cappella—without musical accompaniment. Grandparents and family members filled the gymnasium for the musical program prior to visiting the students' classrooms. Mrs. Hughes's parents happened to be among the crowd in the bleachers. When tiny little Britney belted out her rendition of the "Star Spangled Banner," those sitting nearby remarked that she surely must be lip-synching to a recording. Mrs. Hughes's

The original 1950s cast of the Mickey Mouse Club, with Walt Disney in center. In 1988 Britney auditioned to become a member of a new set of Mousketeers. Although she was unsuccessful on her first try, her audition led to new opportunities in New York City.

parents were quick to inform them that it truly was the little girl's own voice.

No one could believe such a big voice could come from such a little girl.

By the time Britney was a fourth grader, she had her sights set on becoming a part of the troupe on the *Mickey Mouse Club* (*MMC*). This television show first started back in the 1950s. The kids on the original show wore Mouseketeer hats (beanies with ears) and performed a variety of song and dance numbers. In 1988 the Disney marketing people decided to launch an all-new *MMC* and feature it on the Disney channel. The new show resembled the '50s version only in the basic format of plenty of songs, dances, and skits as well as the famous theme song:

M-I-C—See you real soon.

K-E-Y—Why? Because we like you!

M-O-U-S-E

Britney faithfully watched the fresh faces of the new Mouseketeers and dreamed. In her heart of hearts, she saw herself performing on that show.

A friend of Lynne Spears's learned that auditions for the *MMC* were being held in Atlanta, Georgia. In a whirl of excitement and anticipation, Mom and daughter headed to Georgia to enter Britney in the competition.

By now Britney was used to the pressure of competition, but this was different. This prize meant more to her than anything she'd done so far. Through the grueling pace of tryouts and screen tests, young Britney gave it her best. Amazingly, she was one of six out of more than 600 selected for further consideration. By now her hopes were spinning through the roof— only to come crashing down.

The casting director told her that even though she displayed a good deal of talent and stage presence, they felt she was still too young to be on the show. There was an interesting consolation, however. The casting director saw such potential in Britney that he put her and her mother in contact with a well-known agent in New York City. He also encouraged Britney to live in the Big Apple for a time because that's where things happen in the entertainment industry.

Lynne Spears didn't hesitate for a moment. She and Britney and baby Jamie Lynne packed their clothes and moved to New York City for the summer.

3

ON TO
THE BIG APPLE

In the heart of the theater district, at 1733 Broadway, stood the landmark Broadway Dance Center (BDC). The ground floor entrance featured large plate-glass windows where the dancers could be seen in the studios going through their paces. After opening in 1984, the Center had gained a wide reputation by the time Britney became a student there in 1991. Started by owner and director Allison Ellner-Teitlebaum, the Center was *the* place for actors and actresses, famous and not-so-famous, to attend classes in tap, ballet, and modern dance.

The setup at BDC was different from that of most dance studios. Participants could come to the reception area and sign up for any class that was in session. They could come for a single class or purchase a 10-class card. During the summers, children were allowed to be a part of the adult classes. These were the type of classes that Britney attended during her first summer in New York. There she stretched her talents and increased her knowledge and abilities in the field of dance.

A few blocks south of the Broadway Dance Center, at

A dramatic view of Manhattan from the Empire State Building in New York City. Upon arrival in the Big Apple, Britney not only took dance lessons but also began to receive offers for TV commercials.

328 West 48th Street, was the Professional Performing Arts School (PPAS). The facility, which
had opened in 1990, was known for producing
bright talent and new stars. Some of the noted
alumni included Claire Danes (*My So-Called
Life* and *Romeo and Juliet*), and youngest Tony
Award winner for Best Actress, Daisy Egan
(*The Secret Garden*). An extension of the New
York Public School System, PPAS offered
majors in drama, musical theater, theatrical
arts, instrumental music, and dance to students in grades 6 through 12.

The only division open to students Britney's
age was theatrical arts. For her audition, Britney
was required to memorize and perform a two-
minute contemporary monologue, perform a
song a capella that demonstrated her range and
musicianship, perform a dance, and appear
before a panel review. As demanding as it was,
Britney made the cut.

Mornings at PPAS were given over to acade-
mics. At lunch time Britney ate in a cafeteria
shared with a nearby elementary school. Just
after 1:30 P.M. the school switched from acade-
mics to performance classes. Some students
went off-campus to other schools and studios.
Scene Study was held in the auditorium, and
Movement for Singers in the top-floor dance
studio. Young Britney was contented and happy
in this exciting new dream world.

In no time at all Britney and her mother
could navigate around the busy streets of New
York as easily as they could in Kentwood.
Britney took the excitement of the big city right
in stride and wasn't the least bit intimidated.
Her love of traveling and seeing new sights
would come in handy when she would later be
jetting around the world.

The connection with the New York firm that had been recommended proved to be exactly what Britney needed. Offers from ad agencies began to come in. Through the agency's connections, Britney starred in television ads for such companies as Maul's Barbecue and Days Inn. Even more exciting than ads was her opportunity to be scheduled on Ed McMahon's *Star Search* in 1989. On the stage at the New York theater, Britney could do what she loved best—sing and dance. She won the competition in 1989, then turned around and came back the very next year and won again.

Meanwhile, back in McComb, Mississippi, teacher Darlene Hughes sat watching the show. She vividly remembered how, when Mr. McMahon spoke to Britney, the little star politely answered him by saying, "Yes sir," and "No sir." Her strict upbringing was standing her in good stead.

After national television, what more exciting opportunity could come to a girl like Britney than the off-Broadway stage? At last the casting for *Ruthless* was completed and Britney won a spot in the musical comedy spoof. Now she could add the word "actress" to her growing list of credits.

Ruthless is the story of a stagestruck little girl named Tina Denmark who is determined to get the lead in her school play. So determined is Tina that murder is not out of the question. When her plan is discovered, Tina is sent to a "home for the stagestruck," while all the other crazy characters vie to become stars. There are a number of funny twists and turns in the plot, lit up by jokes about show business and famous quotes from famous plays.

"I was playing this really bad child," Britney

Britney takes a break in her dressing room. No stranger to the back-stage life, she appeared in Ruthless, *an off-Broadway musical, for six months in 1992.*

said about the part, "who seems real sweet but she's evil too. It was so much fun!"

Ruthless received rave reviews during its long run. It received a New York Outer Circle Critics Award for Best Off-Broadway Musical. Britney was part of the show for six months.

There were also quiet times in Britney's life. The following summer when her friend, Robbey Hughes, turned 10, Britney was at the Hughes's home for a birthday party beside the pool. The Hughes family treasures the photo of the two girls sitting side-by-side, having a good time together. And Robbey still has the gift Britney gave her—a soft furry teddy bear holding a picture frame.

In the spring of 1992, Britney entered the Miss Talent USA contest held in Monroe, Louisiana, in the northern part of the state. In spite of fierce competition, Britney brought home the 58-inch trophy. This particular trophy would not fit on the shelf with the others. Her newest addition would have to sit on the floor.

With all these accomplishments added to Britney's list of credits, the time had come to once again try out for the *Mickey Mouse Club*. In spite of all that had happened, the dream of becoming a Mouseketeer was still very much alive in her heart.

In the spring of 1993, 15,000 youngsters from 13 cities in the United States and Canada were trying out for only seven available spots on the show. That added up to incredible odds. This time Britney tried out in New York City, which had become like her own home turf. Unlike the first *MMC* tryout, she had more experience now and was familiar with the procedure. She was able to concentrate completely on doing her best as she went through the three days of screen tests.

When the phone call came informing her she was an official Mouseketeer, all Britney could do was scream. Jumping up and down, she was yelling, "I'm so excited! I'm so excited!"

She had dared to dream, and her dream had come true at last. Sounding like a veteran at the young age of 11 she stated, "It was all I'd really wanted since I was eight!"

4

BRITNEY RECEIVES
HER EARS

Britney was one of the seven new cast members who would join the 13 existing members to make up a cast of 20 kids in the *Mickey Mouse Club*. Cast members came from a wide variety of backgrounds and ethnic origins, but all had show business in their blood. Britney was more than ready to be a part of the group.

"When you go to school . . . here," she told a reporter from the *New Orleans Times Picayune*, "none of the people are like you. In Orlando all the kids are like you; they'll do all the stuff you do."

For a youngster who had already met Donald Trump and Macaulay Culkin's family, and had ridden several times in a stretch limousine, it was obvious she wasn't like most of the neighborhood kids in Kentwood. According to Lynne Symons, director of original programming for the Disney Channel, Britney Spears was loaded with talent.

"We require a lot from our cast members," Symons said when Britney was selected for the cast, "acting, singing, dancing, and the indefinable fourth quality of personality. Britney had all four requirements."

The center of the Magic Kingdom at Disney World, where Britney earned her "ears" as a member of the new Mickey Mouse Club. After taping at the MMC studios in the mornings, cast members could enjoy the Magic Kingdom for free in the afternoons.

When Britney's mom was asked about her daughter's success, Lynne Spears said, "This is the most unplanned thing you've ever seen in your life. It was as though I was mindless and things just happened."

Once again it was time to pack up and move. This time, mom, little sister, and Britney would live in Orlando, Florida, close to Disney World, where the rehearsals and tapings would take place. From May through October, Dad again stayed behind with brother Bryan. At Parklane, Britney's classmates celebrated with a going-away party and presented her with a special t-shirt which each of them had signed.

The uprooting was no problem for Britney. "I'm always wanting to get up and go," she said. "Lots of times, I'll be home and just sitting there watching TV and I'll be wishing I was on an airplane to New York or Los Angeles or Florida."

This was the sixth season of the all-new *Mickey Mouse Club.* "It was a lot of fun because I was like a baby," Britney related. "I was 11 and was the youngest one on the show, so people catered to me. Just being in Disney World was a lot of fun."

The pace for the *MMC* troupe was what Britney would later call "laid back." It wasn't at all a "star" lifestyle, but it was certainly what she loved doing. They had set schedules and did the same things each day. "We'd go to the studios in the mornings and we'd get in for free. Then we'd get to go to Disney World alone." Her favorite attraction at Disney World was Space Mountain.

Talking about her new girlfriends whom she met and worked with in the club, she said, "We were like sisters. We talked on the phone and

The cast of the Mickey Mouse Club *with Britney at front right. Besides Britney, quite a few members of the* MMC *later became famous actors and singers.*

acted stupid." Among those friends were Keri Russell, who would later star on the television series *Felicity*, and Christina Aguilera, who would later become a recording star.

J.C. Chasez was already on the show when Britney arrived; Justin Timberlake was a new addition the year Britney came. These boys were destined to become members of the singing group 'N Sync, and Britney's path would cross with theirs again at a later date. During her first *MMC* season she was involved in a wide variety of production numbers. In one number entitled "I Feel for You," she sang the lead with Justin.

When Disney issued some of the first public relations materials on Britney during the sixth season, they described her as "bursting with talent and experience." Her future goals were listed as "attending college and later becoming a professional singer or entertainment lawyer." Her motto to the *MMC* viewers was, "Life is short, don't waste it." Her adult-sounding advice was "Be kind and respect the feelings of others."

Britney's parents were insistent that their daughter keep pace with the high standards of Parklane Academy. They didn't want her to get behind in her studies. Although Britney was no longer in Mrs. Hughes's class at Parklane, her former teacher faxed lesson plans to Britney. "Since the school didn't have a fax machine and I did," Darlene Hughes said, "I took the things home from the other teachers and used my fax to keep Britney updated."

Coming back to Parklane Academy after a session with other child performers wasn't easy. But her music teacher, Mrs. Chamberlin, said Britney worked hard to fit in. Britney never used her show business experiences as a way to show off. While Mrs. Chamberlin wanted to recognize Britney and put her in front as much as possible, Britney wouldn't have it.

Calling her teacher aside, the young performer said, "Mrs. Chamberlin, please don't ask me to sing in front of the other students." Britney wanted to be liked for who she was, rather than what she could do. She didn't want to be singled out.

In May of her sixth-grade year, it was back to Orlando once again. Britney could hardly wait to see her old friends and get back into the things she loved the most—singing, dancing, and performing.

During the seventh season, an interview appeared featuring Britney and her friend Christina Aguilera. When Christina was asked what she liked about Britney, she said, "She can always make me smile and feel good about myself." And when asked to describe Britney in only three words, Christina said, "Cheerful, innocent, and cute!" Both girls commented on how they loved to do things together, such as shopping and going to movies.

In addition to their TV work, the *MMC* members sang in live concerts and cut albums in a fully outfitted recording studio. Each member also received personalized voice lessons. This was the point at which Britney knew this was what she wanted for her life. "I was just in love with music," she recalled. "That's when I realized, I want to go for this!"

That next fall, 1994, when the six-month period of rehearsals and taping had been completed, the sad news was given to the Mouseketeers that the show had been canceled. The moment was a solemn one. All of them knew their fun times together in Orlando were over. Not just for a season, but forever.

In her room back in Kentwood Britney hung her club jacket in the closet and placed several framed pictures of herself and the club members on her walls and dresser. Those photos and the videos of all the episodes would remind her of the wonderful friends she had made and the exciting times she had had during the two fun-filled years.

5

CALM BEFORE
THE STORM

There was nothing to do but return home to Kentwood, to Parklane, and to normalcy. But what was normal? Britney's singing during this quiet time included the church choir, a few weddings, and civic gatherings such as the Lions Club.

At school she donned her number-25 jersey and played girls' basketball. She was an attendant at the prom, and even had a steady boyfriend named Reg. It was all good, but she had to admit she was totally bored.

"It was fun for a while," she said, "but I started getting itchy to get out again and see the world."

It was then that her father contacted Laurence H. Rudolph, an entertainment lawyer, in his second-floor Park Avenue complex in New York City. Rudolph was a founding partner of Rudolph and Beer, an entertainment and general practice law firm. The firm's expertise centered around music, film, television, and sports. Rudolph's job was to counsel recording artists, songwriters, record labels, production companies, publishers, managers, and producers. He was referred to by the press as a "high-powered New York entertainment lawyer."

Britney models sunglasses in a relaxed moment between tours. As part of her 1998 promotional tour, Sunglass Hut offered customers CDs containing one of Britney's songs.

Britney's father had heard that Rudolph was a person who knew what was going on in the industry at any given time. Rudolph told Jamie Spears, "Pop music is coming back. Send me a tape of Britney singing."

At the time an audition was being held for an all-girl vocal group. The girls' quintet, under the name *Innosense*, was formed when Lynn Harless, showbiz mom of Justin Timberlake, decided to manage her own group. Britney was asked to prepare a demo tape for the group, which she did. That was when Rudolph heard her voice and everything changed. He vetoed the group idea altogether because he believed that Britney should follow through with a solo career. He was so impressed with what he heard on the demo, he immediately sent the tape to Jeff Fenster, vice president at Jive Records.

"I got a one-song demo from her [Britney's] manager, Larry Rudolph," Fenster recounted. "She sang over an instrumental that wasn't in her key—but I heard something special. Her vocal ability and commercial appeal caught me right away."

Fenster went on to elaborate, "It's very rare to hear someone that age who can deliver emotional content and commercial appeal. For any artist, the motivation . . . is extremely important. And Britney had that. This is clearly a self-motivated person from a very young age."

The next step was for Britney to audition at Jive Records. She was pretty nervous when she learned she must perform in front of 10 Jive executives. She chose to sing a song of Whitney Houston's, "I Have Nothing." Jive signed her right on the spot!

Once the contracts were signed, it was time to choose Britney's "sound." Several ideas were tossed around, but the record company settled on pop. That made sense because it allowed Britney to do what she did best—dance along with the peppy music.

Prior to Britney's signing on with Jive, the main pop sound had been with boy groups. New Kids on the Block were the sensation in the 1980s. Following closely behind them came Hanson, the Backstreet Boys, and more recently 'N Sync. Also fitting in the list was the Latin-flavored C-Note, 98 Degrees, and 5ive—all boys.

Other than Brandy, Tiffany, and the Spice Girls, the presence of girls on the pop scene was slim. The newest sound coming from the United Kingdom in 1998 was a trio calling themselves Cleopatra. The sisters, Zainam, Cleopatra, and Yonah were making such waves in Britain that there was no time for them to duplicate their success in the United States. The Divine Trio out of New York also came onto the scene in 1998. However their sound was rhythm-and-blues and soul rather than pop. It was into this parade of groups—mostly boys—that Britney arrived as a solo production.

An article from the *Yahoo Daily News* stated that "perhaps . . . the pop market . . . was ripe for a solo star after a parade of groups." The article was right on target.

Jive Records hooked Britney up with producers Eric Foster and Max Martin. By April, Britney was winging her way across the Atlantic to Sweden, which was her first trip overseas. On Kungscholmen Street in Stockholm is Cheiron Studios, made famous by its production of a number of hits such as "The Sign" for Ace of Base, and "Do You Know What it Takes" for Robyn. At Cheiron, Britney met Martin and they set to work.

The Spice Girls were among the only girl groups on the pop music scene in the late 1990s. Britney's star may have risen more quickly because audiences were ready for a solo star after a steady stream of groups.

Because the studio was filled with talented writers and producers, there was no shortage of material. Max Martin and his partner, Swedish mega-producer Denniz PoP, were responsible for nearly all of the hits by Backstreet Boys and 'N Sync. Sadly, the famous 35-year-old PoP had died of cancer in August 1998. Cheiron Studios had been Denniz PoP's own studio. For Britney, stepping into Cheiron was like stepping into musical history.

Britney admits she didn't get to see much of Sweden because "I was in the booth the whole time." The original plan was for Britney to cut three songs in 10 days. Instead, everyone worked so well together they ended up doing half the album at Cheiron. "We got a lot of work done," Britney said, "and I was happy with that."

She said later that she wasn't sure they had a hit until she heard Martin's "Baby One More Time." "I was totally flattered Max Martin would allow me to sing that song."

When the sessions at Cheiron were done, it was back to the United States. The remainder of the album was recorded at Battery Studios in New York City with Eric Foster White, who produced and wrote material for Boyzone, Hi-Five, and Whitney Houston. By July the album was finished.

"It came together rather quickly—unusually so for a pop album," Fenster said. "It was a case of good chemistry among a group of very talented people. The writers and producers immediately saw what we at the label did: Britney is a star."

In describing her sessions with Max Martin and Eric Foster White, Britney said the famous producers were "really sweet and down-to-earth guys. You can talk to them about anything. It was a great experience to work with them."

With barely a chance to catch her breath, Britney's attention was turned to the production of the video. While still in New York City, Britney met with the video producers and she immediately disagreed with their production ideas for the *Baby One More Time* video shoot. Their plan, she said, was "off the wall." Once she presented her ideas of a school scene, and after her ideas had been accepted, the obvious choice of setting was Venice High School. After a few dance rehearsals in New York, it was time to catch a plane for the West Coast. Britney quickly fell in love with the warmth and sunshine in Los Angeles.

Once the album and video were in place, Jive Records set up a Britney Spears website, E-mail address, and toll-free number. This information was printed up on several hundred thousand postcards and sent off to various teen fan clubs around the nation. The web page featured photos, videotaped interview footage, and music clips. This served as the kickoff for a huge promo blitz.

In late July 1998, almost six months before the release of the record, Britney traveled across the nation and into Canada, performing at 28 different shopping malls. The blitz was much like the one Debbie Gibson, the teen singing star of the '80s, had done in her era.

The North American promotional tour was sponsored by several teen magazines such as *YM, Teen, Seventeen,* and *Teen People.* If that weren't enough, a Sunglass Hut tie-in capped it off. With a purchase of $80 or more at Sunglass Hut, shoppers received a free CD containing one of Britney's songs.

The musical mall program included a four-song set performed in the food courts with two dancers accompanying Britney. Kim Kaiman, Jive's marketing director, said of Britney, "We knew we had this great package—a gifted singer who could also dance like a dream. We knew people would go for her once they saw her."

After the song and dance numbers, the troupe handed out goody bags containing cassette samplers. Britney found herself signing autographs even before the album was released. Kaiman reported that the blitz was a great success. "The response was tremendous," she said. "Kids were intrigued by Britney."

Kaiman was impressed with Britney's cheerfulness during the grueling tour. "I've never seen an artist so focused on what she needed to do," Kaiman commented. The tour also included plenty of radio interview spots. "One of the reasons that radio fell in love with her," Kaiman explained, "is that she's so very southern, so sweet and gracious."

Britney's powerful voice gets regular workouts. When she was recording her first album in studios in Sweden and New York, Britney spent day after day in the recording booth, with little time to do anything but sing.

Being on the road meant Britney studied on the plane and in her hotel room. A tutor traveled with her, and all her tests were sent to the University of Nebraska, where her home-schooling courses were based. "It's very hard to stay disciplined," she admitted. "It's easy to wait too long to do your homework." She also added that she needed a "lot of help with geometry and Spanish."

A friend of the family, Felicia Culotta, became Britney's adult traveling companion on the

Britney signs an autograph for a fan in San Francisco. During her grueling—but highly successful—tour of malls throughout the country, Britney was always gracious to fans and humble about her newfound success.

road. The 30-something Culotta was a person the family could trust; thus Lynne could stay home and continue teaching and be a wife and mother. But that didn't mean she stopped being concerned about her world-traveling daughter.

"I worry about her terribly," her mother admitted candidly to *People* magazine. "But I'm so much happier knowing she's doing what she really wants to."

The mall tour turned out to be an overwhelming success. "It went over like gangbusters," Kaiman announced, "drawing hundreds of kids in every market." Before the tour was even completed, Britney received word she was being offered the spot of opening act on a tour with 'N Sync. This was the group in which two of her former Mouseketeer buddies, Justin Timberlake and J.C. Chasez, were a part. She was thrilled. After cutting only one album, she was being offered a national tour. It seemed almost too good to be true.

The commercial release for the album was slated for October 1998. This meant the CD was sent out to radio stations across the country. The first time Britney heard her own song on the radio, it was an unforgettable experience. She'd just come back from one of her trips and was on her way home from the airport when it came on the air. In Britney's words, "It goobed me! . . . It was cool. It was the best feeling."

All of a sudden, coming back home to Kentwood was a little different. She and her cousin Laura Lynn Wall could still go to the Sonic for something to eat, and they still went to the movies together, but now more people were coming up to Britney to talk and ask questions. Some offered their congratulations; others told her how happy they were for her. Many wanted her autograph. The little girls asked if Britney would give them singing lessons.

Things were indeed changing very quickly. It looked as though Britney's boring days at home in Kentwood, Louisiana, were fading into the distance.

6

TO THE
TOP

By the time Britney's single, "Baby One More Time," was released in November, there were hundreds of Internet websites dedicated to photos and detailed information about Britney Spears. Suddenly everyone wanted to know everything about her. Young Web surfers were taking notice of this rising star. "You can't dictate to kids," Kim Kaiman remarked about Britney's exploding popularity, "they're independent buyers." And the kids were buying Britney's music.

The tour with 'N Sync meant exchanging jet planes for a tour bus. On the bus were Britney's four dancers (two guys and two gals), the tour manager, the hair stylist, the bus driver, Britney's traveling companion, Felicia, and of course, Britney. "My dancers have been on bus tours before," she wrote in an E-mail to her fans, "and have taught us some really fun 'bus games.' I laugh so hard 'til my belly hurts the next day." She added that she hadn't yet mastered the art of sleeping on the bus.

Britney confessed she was quite nervous at her first

On tour, Britney always dazzles fans with her high-energy numbers. On her tour with 'N Sync she was nervous at first about opening for a group of boys in front of crowds of girls. But she quickly won over her audiences, who often danced enthusiastically along with the music.

'N Sync performs in concert. When Britney opened for the popular boy band, the primarily female audience, although initially disappointed, were soon won over by her spirit and energy.

concert on the tour. She wasn't sure how a crowd of girls would react to having a girl come out for the opening act for 'N Sync. "I was worried about the girls having that jealousy with me opening up . . . and them loving the guys. They might think, 'Who is this girl? Get off the stage. I wanna see 'N Sync!'"

There was a smattering of boos at some places; however, Britney's confidence and her talent quickly won over the young concertgoers.

One enthusiastic new fan wrote the following review:

> Britney Spears was no stranger to the crowd and her set showed us she's also no flash in the pan. Performing a handful of cuts from her just-released album, Britney had everyone up on their feet and screaming—I mean dancing—along. She closed with her smash "Baby One More Time," which not only was the most polished performance of her set but also brought her a standing ovation.

By the end of November, there was hardly a teen magazine that didn't have an article or at least a picture of Britney featured in it. Some analysts compared her success to the rise of Debbie Gibson, but she countered those comments by saying, "My music is totally different." And of course every romantically minded young person wanted to link her to Justin Timberlake, especially since she was on tour with 'N Sync. The truth was she rarely saw the boys. They were on separate tour buses and had different rehearsal times. "They're just like big brothers to me," she was forced to say repeatedly. Her fans couldn't understand that at present there just wasn't any time in her life for a romantic relationship.

Sharing her thoughts about relationships, Britney has said, "I want a guy who can be totally honest with me and make me laugh." Because she is on the road much of the time, she feels "there would have to be a major amount of trust." When asked who would be her fantasy dinner date, Britney put Brad Pitt high on her list.

Britney was hot. With all of the exposure she was getting, a rash of offers were coming her way, one of which was to sign on as a model for Tommy Hilfiger. Another offer was for her to become the 1999 spokesperson for the *Just Nikki* catalog.

When Britney turned 17 on December 2, she was in Kalamazoo, Michigan. The troupe went to a restaurant, and with silly hats, balloons, and a cake, they celebrated her birthday. One great birthday present was the fact that her single was climbing up the charts. It was number 9 on *Billboard's* Hot 100 List. The video was on top of the charts on The Box and had entered a rotation on MTV. Invitations began to come in for TV appearances such as *Box Talk* and *The Howie Mandell Show.*

On the bus, J.T., their devoted driver, surprised the troupe by decorating the entire back lounge with strings and strings of colored Christmas lights. As Britney put it, "We now have a real Christmas room (on the bus)!" Meanwhile Britney found time for a little shopping. She'd purchased gifts for her family and was looking forward to being at Kentwood for the holidays. "I bought my sister this big stocking," she told reporters, "and filled it with cute pajamas from the Limited."

The quiet break at Christmas—with brother Bryan home from Southeastern Louisiana University—was all too short. While Britney admitted she didn't actually get homesick on the road, she did miss her family, her room, and her own bed. "I'm such a homey person," she said to John Norris of *MTV News.* "I have everything where it's supposed to be and . . . I love going into my room."

The "everything" Britney referred to included a massive collection of dolls. Every year for Christmas she received a new doll, and her small bedroom was overflowing with them. The newest addition was a collector doll that she said reminded her of her grandmother.

Pleased as she was to be back home, Britney was not really looking for a rest. She was tremendously excited to be back on stage, in the spotlights, doing exactly what she loved to do most.

When Britney was once asked what she thought the best part of being famous was, she answered, "Getting to travel and see the world, and performing, and knowing all those people out there know the words to your song. . . . It's the best feeling in the world."

On January 12 the *Baby One More Time* album was officially released. Britney was in West Palm Beach, Florida, fast asleep, when Larry Rudolph called her from New York. With him on the conference call was Jeff Fenster from Jive. Britney was groggy with sleep when they asked her, "Are you sitting down? Are you ready for this?" That's when they both announced to her, at the same time, that her debut album entered the chart as number one.

"I totally flipped," she told an MTV interviewer, "It was really awesome."

Suddenly Britney was breaking all kinds of chart records. She had just become the first new female artist to have a simultaneous number-one single and a number-one album on the *Billboard* charts.

Now a lot more attention was being focused on Britney, and most all her reviews were favorable. *CD Now*'s analysis of her abilities noted that "with obvious influence from Mariah Carey, she [Britney] glides quite ably through the key changes and delivers octave leaps and vibratos that should melt just about any heart, young or old."

During one of her stage performances, a special person was watching from backstage. His name was Johnny Wright. Johnny and his wife Donna were the managers for 'N Sync. A few years earlier the Wrights had been instrumental in successfully launching the Backstreet Boys. Johnny liked what he saw and heard of Britney at the concert. "I saw how talented Britney was, but I also saw there was more development needed," he reluctantly confessed. Before the month was out, he signed on to Spears's team.

At the time, Britney wasn't sure whether Larry Rudolph was the manager and Johnny the co-manager, or the other way around. But it didn't matter. As she put it, "It works out really well."

When asked about all the things she had to sacrifice for her life on the road, Britney assured the media that she wasn't giving anything up. "If I wasn't in love with my job and in love with music," she said, "I would be homesick and going crazy." As it was, she was enjoying every minute!

On January 16 the tour took Britney close to home with a concert at Baton Rouge. Many familiar home folk were in the crowd, including Darlene Hughes. While the throng of young people screamed and clapped and sang to the music, Darlene sat there with tears of joy streaming down her cheeks as she remembered the cute and lovable little girl who'd been in her

third-grade class at Parklane.

In the midst of the good things that were happening, a sour note suddenly sounded. On January 20 a producer from Philadelphia, William Kahn, filed a complaint against Britney, her parents, Larry Rudolph, and the Jive Record Company. Kahn claimed he was the one who had launched Britney's career. And indeed he had been her manager for a short time. He was demanding more than $75,000 for his percentage of commission. By February the suit had been settled out of court by Rudolph's efficient law firm. In spite of that, the incident upset Britney, and she was thankful when it was cleared up.

The 'N Sync tour came to a close at the end of January. "It's been an incredible, intense

Mariah Carey and Whitney Houston, Britney's favorite singing stars, whose songs she used to mimic as a child. Now Britney is being compared to them in her talent and style.

time," Britney said of the tour. "It hasn't always been easy opening for these guys, since there are all girls in the audience. But I ultimately am able to win them over. I have guy dancers, too—and believe me that helps."

Now it was time for Britney to turn her attention to a new single, "Sometimes." This song, according to Britney, was "about a girl who really likes a guy but is shy and doesn't know how to approach him."

While at the New York City studio rehearsing for a video shoot, Britney was in a room by herself warming up for the dance scenes. As she had done hundreds of times before, she performed a high kick with her right leg. As she did, her left knee twisted in a wrong direction and totally gave out. She fell to the floor. She had already been chiding herself for failing to practice her dancing on a daily basis, and then "like a goof, I twisted my knee!"

Suddenly Britney's busy life came to a standstill. The video shoot was postponed, and several TV appearances were canceled. She was scheduled for photo shoots for *Entertainment Weekly* along with the guys from 'N Sync. They had planned for the troupe to form a human pyramid for the shots. That plan was scrapped when Britney showed up in her knee brace.

At first the doctors weren't sure how bad the injury was, but after a few days, surgery was scheduled. A small scope was used so no incision was required. The doctors informed Britney that she was lucky she didn't tear any ligaments. Following the surgery, she was instructed to give it time to heal. That meant heading back home to Kentwood.

During this much-needed rest, Britney made

it a point to E-mail all her fans. In the letter she said, "I like meeting all the kids [in my travels] because it's like making new friends all over the world. I feel really lucky that I can do this, and every time I meet someone who tells me they like my music, it makes me feel really good. . . . I hope this never ends."

One good thing did come from her recuperation time. A scheduled interview and photo shoot with *Rolling Stone* magazine was done at Parklane Academy and at the Spears home in Kentwood, rather than in a studio. This meant

Adoring fans cheer Britney at all her public appearances. She has said that she loves meeting fans wherever she goes because it is like making new friends all over the world.

that Britney's younger sister, Jamie Lynne, and older brother, Bryan, had their photos in the popular magazine as well.

At the school, the kids were preparing to perform one of Mrs. Chamberlin's famous musicals. This year it was *Annie*. Mrs. Chamberlin's son, Monte, had just had his head shaved for the role of Daddy Warbucks in the play. When the people from *Rolling Stone* saw a student with his head shaved, they immediately cornered him and talked him into posing shirtless in the photos with *I Love Britney* written on his chest, and with the now-famous pink pompoms glued to his head. (Britney had worn similar ones in her *Baby One More Time* video.) The sight of Monte with no shirt brought a good laugh to the student body at Parklane, since they observe a strict dress code.

There was also another important person starring in Parklane's spring musical production that year. That was Jamie Lynne Spears, Britney's younger sister. Jamie Lynne played one of the orphans.

Darlene Hughes was in the audience at the theater in McComb on the opening night of *Annie*. Just before the lights dimmed, Britney slipped in almost unnoticed through a side door—still on crutches—and sat with her family right in front of Darlene.

Things were a little different now than they had been; Britney was not able to come and go as freely as she once had. Lynne Spears knew the paparazzi were following her daughter constantly. At this point in Britney's career even European tabloid news reporters attempted to get photos of her.

During the intermission, a few kids saw

Britney and came asking for autographs. "She didn't turn anybody away," Darlene said. "She talked to everyone who came to her whether she knew them or not."

As the final curtain fell, Britney gathered her crutches and stood up. She turned to give her former teacher a hug and whispered. "I'm going to scoot out this door. I'm not here for me; I just came to see my little sister."

As Darlene later explained, "Britney could have had all kinds of attention brought to her, but she chose not to. She left for the right reasons." And then she added softly, "She's so sweet!"

WHAT
NEXT?

*D*awson's Creek is a television show set in the country-side near Boston. The story line centers on a 15-year-old named Dawson Leery, played by teen heartthrob James Van Der Beek. Four teens who have been best friends since childhood are entering the confusing time of adolescence.

In March 1999 it was announced that Britney Spears had been signed to perform in a three-episode story for the spring 2000 season. Columbia TriStar TV, which is responsible for the show, also talked to Britney about eventually starring in her own drama or comedy.

According to Larry Rudolph, Britney was not interested in doing a sitcom, but Columbia TriStar TV just happened to produce the kind of dramas Britney would like to do. In a statement to *Entertainment Weekly*, Britney insisted, "I won't play somebody mean, and I won't play myself." And so far Britney has had final say.

The journey from Miss Donewar's Dance School in Kentwood, Louisiana, to stages in London and Singapore may seem like a long one. Britney's career is still sky-rocketing. Where she goes from this point no one knows,

---

Britney at a Toronto department store during her 1999 Canadian concert tour. The tour is only the beginning of a busy year for the teen star; her future plans include acting in three episodes of the popular TV show Dawson's Creek.

but many try to guess. The media attempt to project what she might do next, and predict whether her fame will last or burn out like a shooting star.

"Here's a girl," said manager Johnny Wright, "who basically went from nowhere to number one overnight. The Backstreet Boys and 'N Sync," he continued, "had time to develop, to work on performing . . . before all the pressure came down. What's going on with Britney right now is she's just getting bombarded."

Jeff Fenster wasn't worried. He had faith in Britney's abilities. "I think she's got the opportunity to become someone who combines the best elements of Madonna . . . with the serious singers she looks up to: the Whitney Houstons and Celine Dions."

According to Britney herself, most all her future plans include music. Part of that plan was to begin writing songs. The B-side of the single "Sometimes" featured a song called "I'm So Curious," with melody and lyrics penned by Britney Spears. Surely more will follow.

"I want music to always be a part of my life . . . and I want to grow as a person each time each album comes out."

Another future desire of Britney's is to help disabled children. "They have such happy spirits inside," she told a Cleveland reporter. "I'd like to go to hospitals and touch lives."

Britney is also very aware of her responsibility as a role model to younger kids. "You want to be a good example for kids out there and not do something stupid," she said. "Kids have low self-esteem, and then the peer pressures come and they go into a wrong crowd. That's when all the bad stuff starts happening, drugs and stuff. I think if they find something

that keeps them happy—writing, drawing, anything like that—they'll have confidence." In her comments to her fans and to the press, Britney continually encourages young people to follow their dreams.

Britney is often described by the media as a "nice girl." One reporter wrote that, "Britney Spears is so nice it's almost disturbing. She's really just one big ball of nice-itude."

Another article described her as "unintimidating." The writer went on to say, "Preteens want to identify with her, and can envision themselves with Britney . . . as their best girlfriend. She's the teenybopper all young girls want to have a sleepover with."

Will success spoil this niceness? Or more importantly, will success spoil Britney? Her

Britney always has a smile and a wave for her fans. Despite her meteoric rise to fame, Britney remains a cheerful, down-to-earth person who is unspoiled by success.

mom doesn't think so. Years earlier when Britney first made it into the *Mickey Mouse Club*, her mother commented, "There're a lot of kids that this would ruin, but I feel sure that this will make an even better person out of Britney." Then she added, "Britney could win the Academy Award in three different movies and she would still have a humble spirit."

Britney is already winning awards. At the inagural Teen Choice Awards in August 1999, Britney introduced the show and went on to win Single of the Year with "Baby One More Time." She was also nominated for several MTV Video Music Awards in the categories Best Pop Video, Best Female Video, and Best Choreography in a Video for her debut single.

The little girl with the big voice and the big dreams may just prove her mom to be right!

CHRONOLOGY

1981	Born on December 2 to Jamie and Lynne Spears in Kentwood, Louisiana.
1984	Begins dance lessons.
1986	Enters Parklane Academy.
1989	Tries out first time for *Mickey Mouse Club*; moves to New York City for the summer; attends dance classes at Broadway Dance Center and Professional Performing Art School; appears in TV commercials.
1989–90	Wins *Star Search* competition two years in a row.
1992	Appears in off-Broadway musical, *Ruthless*.
1993–94	Joins the cast of the all-new *Mickey Mouse Club*.
1995–97	Shows demo tape to Jive Records executives; audits at Jive; signs contract with Jive.
1998	Makes *Baby One More Time* album and video; performs at 28 shopping malls to promote the album; tours with 'N Sync.
1999	*Baby One More Time* album released; both album and single become number one on the *Billboard* charts; films video *Sometimes*; makes television appearances; tours Canada and the United States; films video *(You Drive Me) Crazy*; wins Teen Choice Award for Single of the Year for "Baby One More Time."

ACCOMPLISHMENTS

Discography

1998   *Sabrina the Teenage Witch* (soundtrack)

1999   *Baby One More Time* (album and video)

Theater

1992   *Ruthless*

Television

1989-90   *Star Search* (two-time winner)

1993–94   *Mickey Mouse Club* (cast member)

Guest Appearances

All That
American Music Awards
Dini
Donnie & Marie
Electric Circus
Grind All Over
The Howie Mandel Show
MTV Pre-Grammy Show
Motown Live
Much Music
Rosie O'Donnell Show
Total Request Live
YTV's Hit List

Commercials

Bell South
Days Inn
Maul's Barbecue Sauce

FURTHER READING

Greenberg, Keith Elliot. *New Kids On The Block.* Minneapolis: Lerner Publications, 1991.

Hinz, Martin. *Louisiana.* New York: Children's Press, 1998.

Jones, Bill T. *Dance.* New York: Hyperion Books for Children, 1998.

Lovett, Sarah. *Kidding Around New York: A Young Person's Guide.* Santa Fe, NM: J. Muir Publications, 1993.

Powers, Bill. *Behind the Scenes of a Broadway Musical.* New York: Crown Publishers, 1982.

Santoli, Lorraine. *The Official Mickey Mouse Book.* New York: Hyperion, 1995.

ABOUT THE AUTHOR

NORMA JEAN LUTZ, who lives in Tulsa, Oklahoma, has been writing professionally since 1977. She is the author of more than 250 short stories and articles as well as 36 books—fiction and non-fiction. Of all the writing she does, she most enjoys writing children's books.

INDEX